LULU GOES
TO WITCH SCHOOL

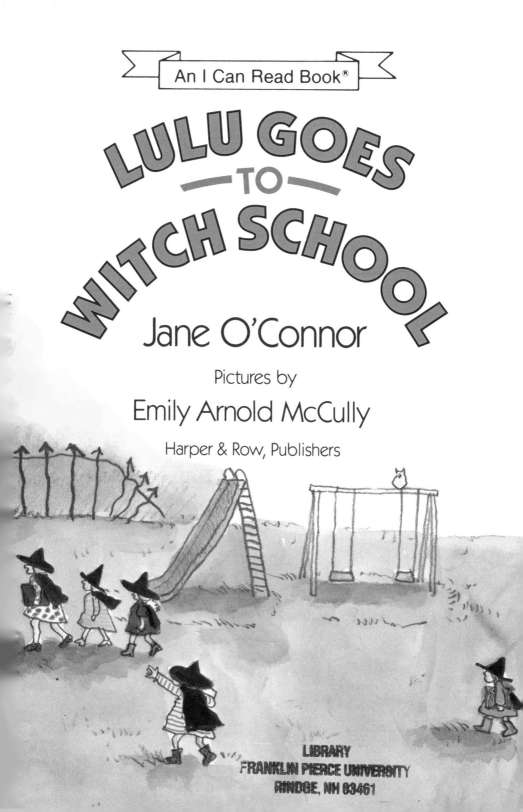

An I Can Read Book®

LULU GOES
—TO—
WITCH SCHOOL

Jane O'Connor

Pictures by

Emily Arnold McCully

Harper & Row, Publishers

Library of Congress Cataloging-in-Publication Data
O'Connor, Jane.
    Lulu goes to witch school.

    (An I can read book)
    Summary: Lulu starts witch school and meets a
classmate who is best at everything.
    [1. Witches—Fiction.   2. Schools—Fiction]
I. McCully Emily Arnold, ill.   II. Title.   III. Series.
PZ7.0222Lv   1987   [E]   87-37
ISBN 0-06-024628-6
ISBN 0-06-024629-4 (lib. bdg.)

For Jim

It was the first day

of witch school.

Lulu Witch was happy.

She was scared, too.

She had never been

to witch school before.

Lulu could not eat

her frosted snake flakes.

She felt as if bats

were inside her tummy.

7

Part of Lulu wished

she was little, like Witch Baby.

Part of Lulu wished

she was staying home

with Mama Witch too.

Lulu got her new broom

and her lunch box

with Dracula on it.

"Good-bye," she called.

Mama Witch kissed Lulu Witch.

Witch Baby waved bye-bye.

Lulu walked to witch school

as fast as she could.

She did not want to be late.

Lots of little witches

were going into the witch school.

A big witch stood at the door.

"Hello. I am Miss Slime," she said.

"I am your teacher."

"Hello. I am Lulu Witch," said Lulu.

11

Miss Slime smiled.

She had a long nose

and a wart on her chin.

Lulu thought Miss Slime

was very pretty.

Miss Slime took Lulu

to her classroom.

"Here is your cubbyhole,"

Miss Slime told Lulu.

"It has a picture

of a bat on it.

You can put your broom

and your lunch box here."

12

Lulu sat down at a big table.

A little witch

with curly hair

sat next to her.

14

"Hello. I am Lulu Witch,"
said Lulu.

"Hello. I am Sandy Witch,"
said the little witch with curly hair.

15

"Do you have

your own magic wand?"

"No," said Lulu Witch.

"I do," said Sandy Witch.

"Do you have

your own black cat?"

"Not yet," said Lulu Witch.

"I do," said Sandy Witch.

"Do you have your own broom?"

asked Lulu Witch.

"Of course," said Sandy Witch.

"I got my first broom

when I was three."

Lulu Witch and Sandy Witch

had to stop talking.

Miss Slime was standing

in front of the class.

She told all the little witches

how busy they were going to be

in witch school.

First they sang a song called

"Happy Witches Are We."

Sandy Witch already knew the words.

Then they drew pictures.

Sandy Witch's picture was so good

Miss Slime put it on the wall.

At snack time

Sandy Witch got to pass out

the lizard tarts.

After the little witches

ate their tarts,

Miss Slime told them

to get their brooms.

She was going to show them

how to fly.

Miss Slime and all the little witches

went out into the graveyard.

One by one the little witches

tried to fly on their brooms.

One little witch fell

as soon as she took off.

One little witch bumped into a tree.

One little witch wobbled

up and down.

At last it was Lulu's turn.

Up, up, up she flew.

She did not wobble.

She did not bump into anything.

She even flew backward.

Lulu flew backward

all the way down.

"Very good, Lulu!"

said Miss Slime.

Lulu Witch smiled.

Miss Slime was proud of her!

Then it was Sandy Witch's turn.

Sandy Witch flew backward.

Sandy Witch flew upside down.

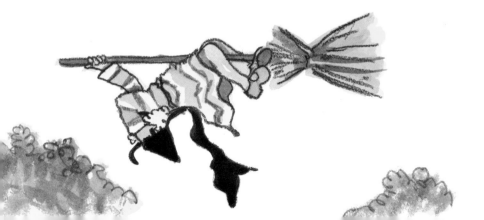

Sandy Witch flew

in a loop-the-loop.

Sandy Witch even flew with no hands!

"Wow!" shouted the little witches.

When Lulu Witch got home,

Mama Witch asked,

"How was witch school?"

"I like my teacher,"

said Lulu Witch.

"But I do not like

one witch in my class.

She is best at everything."

"Maybe you will like her

better tomorrow,"

said Mama Witch.

Lulu Witch did not like
Sandy Witch any better
the next day.

At lunch Sandy Witch said,
"Your rat liver sandwich
looks rotten."
"It does not,"
said Lulu Witch.
"It tastes good."
Sandy Witch looked
at Lulu Witch's sandwich
and held her nose.

She got another little witch

to hold her nose too.

That night Mama Witch asked,

"How was school?"

"I still do not like that witch,"

said Lulu Witch.

"She is mean."

"Then be extra nice to her,"

said Mama Witch.

"It is hard to be mean

when someone is extra nice."

The next day

Lulu Witch said to Sandy Witch,

"Do you want to play with me?"

"Okay," said Sandy Witch.

"We will play

Monster in the Middle.

Lulu is the monster."

Sandy Witch and Hazel Witch

threw a ball back and forth.

Lulu Witch tried to catch it.

But Sandy Witch

always grabbed the ball away.

"Lulu can't catch!

Lulu can't catch!"

Sandy Witch shouted.

Then she bounced the ball

on Lulu's head.

After school

Lulu Witch ran home.

"I was nice,"

she told her mother.

"It did not work.

I do not like that witch at all."

"Do not look so mad,"

said Mama Witch.

"I have a surprise.

I made a new dress for you."

Mama Witch held up the dress.

It was gray with spiders on it.

"Thank you, Mama!"

said Lulu Witch.

"I will wear it

to witch school tomorrow."

The next morning

Miss Slime said,

"That is a very pretty dress."

"Thank you," said Lulu Witch.

Then Miss Slime told the class,

"Today I will teach you

how to spell."

"Hooray!" cried the little witches.

Sandy Witch put up her hand.

"I know how to spell already,"

she said.

"Will you show the class?"

asked Miss Slime.

Sandy Witch stood up.

She got out her magic wand.

"First you close your eyes,"

said Sandy Witch.

"Then you wave your magic wand.

And then you say

the magic words."

Sandy Witch looked right

at Lulu Witch.

Then she closed her eyes.

She waved her magic wand.

She said,

"Hocus-pocus

watercress,

watch me change

old Lulu's dress!"

43

All of a sudden Lulu Witch

felt something go POP!

She looked down at her new dress.

Oh no!

Sandy Witch had changed

the spiders into flowers.

Her new dress looked so ugly now.

Miss Slime saw

that Lulu Witch was mad.

She made Sandy Witch

change the flowers

back into spiders.

But Lulu was still mad.

"I can't stand that little witch,"
Lulu told her mother.
She wished she did not
have to go to witch school.
She wished she never had to see
Sandy Witch again.

The next day Lulu woke up.
Her head hurt.
Her eyes did too.
She went to the mirror.
"Slippery snake guts!"
she shouted.

There were spots—

big red spots—

all over her face.

Lulu ran to find Mama Witch.

"Look at me!" cried Lulu Witch.

"I bet that mean old Sandy Witch

put another spell on me."

48

"No, dear,"

said Mama Witch.

"I am afraid

you have lizard pox!"

49

Mama Witch made Lulu Witch
get back into bed.
"You cannot go
to witch school today,"
Mama Witch told her.
Lulu was glad.

Mama Witch brought Lulu Witch

a big bowl

of dragon noodle soup.

It made Lulu feel better.

Later Mama Witch

read a nice scary story

to Lulu Witch.

The next day

Lulu drew pictures.

She did puzzles

and she played with

her haunted dollhouse.

Was she glad not to see

Sandy Witch!

The day after that

Lulu wanted to fly

her broom outside.

"No, dear,"

said Mama Witch.

"You must stay in the house."

Lulu started to play

with Witch Baby.

"No, dear,"

said Mama Witch.

"I do not want Witch Baby

to catch lizard pox."

"There is nothing

for me to do,"

Lulu Witch said.

She wondered what Miss Slime

and the little witches

were doing at witch school.

The next day

Mama Witch said

Lulu Witch was ready

to go back to witch school.

Deep down Lulu was happy.

She got her broom

and her lunch box

with Dracula on it.

"Good-bye," she called

to Mama Witch and Witch Baby.

Lulu walked to witch school

as fast as she could.

She knew Sandy Witch

was going to make fun of her spots.

But she was not going to get mad.

If the other little witches laughed,

Lulu was going to laugh too.

So there!

Lulu Witch walked into

the classroom.

She put her broom

and her lunch box

in the cubbyhole

with the bat on it.

"Welcome back!" said Miss Slime.

"We missed you."

Lulu sat down

at the big table.

Where was Sandy Witch?

She did not see her.

Then Sandy Witch

came in the door.

There were spots

all over her face!

"You had lizard pox!"

Lulu Witch and Sandy Witch

shouted at the same time.

Sandy Witch sat down

next to Lulu Witch.

"You look funny," said Sandy Witch.

"You do too," said Lulu Witch.

They both laughed.

"I bet I have

more spots than you,"

said Sandy Witch.

"You do not!"

said Lulu Witch.

"We will count and see."

Lulu Witch counted the spots

on Sandy Witch's face.

There were 67.

Then Sandy Witch counted

Lulu's spots.

Lulu had 69!

For once she had done

something better than

Sandy Witch.

"You win,"

said Sandy Witch.

Lulu smiled.

64

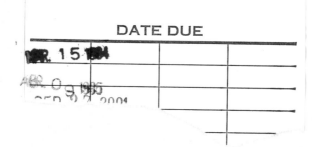